ON SALE

Tracy L. Kinne

authorHOUSE®

AuthorHouse™
1663 Liberty Drive
Bloomington, IN 47403
www.authorhouse.com
Phone: 1-800-839-8640

Published by AuthorHouse 3/14/2012

ISBN: 978-1-4685-5810-4 (sc)
ISBN: 978-1-4685-5809-8 (e)

Library of Congress Control Number: 2012903655

CONTENTS

Chapter 1

THE BEGINNING

I was one of the many professionals in the United States displaced shortly before and during the Great Recession of December 2007 through June 2009. I was a newspaper reporter and editor for 21 years. I took a buyout in June 2007. I figured I had a few options for decent employment. A friend told me his housemate could get me a job at a local chain discount store, if worse came to worst.

Worse came to worst. I started work that September. It was the beginning of a nearly four-year-long, exhausting, depressing odyssey at a chain I'll call Big Box Stores Inc. But I met the most fabulous people I've perhaps ever known. I saw their struggles close up. Some of those struggles I shared -- trying to make ends meet on subsistence hourly wages when the cost of food and energy were rising. At the same time, managers were cutting the number of hours they would let most employees work. When an employee balked, managers lied, told the employee it was his, or her (usually her), fault for not being available to the company 24 hours a day, seven days a week. But if an employee was available 24/7, that employee would find herself, or himself, on an endless swing shift, working 6 a.m. to 2 p.m. one day, then working 6 to 11 p.m. two days later. The days an employee would work also changed weekly. Every once in a great while, a worker would have two days off in a row, unless the worker had to take an extra shift on one of those days to make up for another shift the company had shortened.

For some employees, it wasn't as bad as it was for others. Some employees were retired from their careers and had pensions to fall back on. A few were just there for the health insurance. The widows had trouble; Social Security didn't provide them enough money to live on. The people with children had trouble. Even the people with only dogs had trouble. Every expense, even the most bare, had to be carefully considered. Budgets were tight. I was fortunate; I was single with no dependents and no debt. I lived in a small house that had been paid for in full long ago and drove a reliable vehicle that I owned outright. (Sparse options for public transportation in my rural area made driving practically a necessity.) I had some savings stashed away. I had a 401(k). My health was good. If I pinched my pennies, I hoped, I would be OK, at least until I could figure out some other work arrangement. Many Big Box workers were not as fortunate as I was.

And Big Box, compared with convenience stores and other small chain employers in the area, paid well and had good benefits. Many workers held two jobs. One woman, an emergency medical technician, drove for a local ambulance. She had just switched employment from one ambulance corps, which paid her $9 an hour, to another, which paid $10 an hour. Another, trained as a licensed practical nurse but without the money to take the state licensing exam, worked as a hospital aide for $10.25 an hour. Since both workers had been at Big Box for several years and had accumulated small raises, their Big Box pay was slightly higher. But pay at Big Box, except for salaried managers, was far from good. Yet Big Box, like other chain stores, posted billions of dollars in profit each year. The descendants of the chain's founder were among the wealthiest people in the United States. What has this country come to, I asked myself. How did we let the poor become poorer and the rich become richer during the decades of my life?

My father was a union autoworker during the 1970s. I've plugged his annual pay into an inflation calculator. In my top earning years as a professional with a bachelor's degree, I never made near what he did. He was a high school dropout. Some people say the unions got greedy. I ask, "Who's greedy now?"

One of my coworkers at Big Box had a theory that greed is behind most -- if not all -- of the world's problems. She's one of those amazing people I met at Big Box. Her story deserves to be told. As with all the people from Big Box, I've changed her name and enough details that I hope I can protect her privacy. In many cases, I've combined several people into one character. But the essence of what I'm writing is real. These are true stories. This is America today.

THE CHARACTERS

Kim is the coworker who has the theory regarding greed. She likes to watch documentaries on cable television in the bedroom of her mobile home in a trailer park. Many Big Box employees live in trailers, despite the cold, snowy winters that our region is famous for getting. They can't afford more comfortable housing. And just when the heating bills get high in January is when the company, scaling back after the holiday shopping season ends, cuts employee hours.

Kim doesn't drive. She was a stay-at-home mother whose husband left her after their five children were grown. She's 45. Her coworkers offer to give her rides home, but Kim is proud and independent. It's a little too far to walk, about five miles, especially in the cold of winter or the heat of summer, but her children will usually chauffeur her. She hates to take rides from her coworkers. But nobody minds helping her because Kim is appreciative and is a genuinely warm, caring person.

Kim has had her share of misfortune. She was living with her fiance several years ago when their home caught on fire as they slept one night. A passing motorist saw flames. Kim was pulled from the burning structure. Her fiance was killed in the fire. Kim was hospitalized for three weeks. Her hands were so badly burned that her doctors told her she would never use them again. But Kim, who is stubborn, went to physical therapy and exercised her hands religiously. When I met her, you never would have guessed she had been injured.

While many workers suffer back and knee pain, tendonitis in their forearms and carpel tunnel syndrome in their wrists, Kim credits her work with keeping her hands flexible. She looks at each day as a gift. "I almost lost my life," she told me.

Medicaid covered Kim's hospital and therapy bills because she had no money. But her coworkers at Big Box organized a benefit dinner at a local church where a coworker served as pastor. The money raised helped her family pay incidental costs -- parking fees at the hospital parking garage, clothes and items lost in the fire. The coworkers have a strong sense of community and are generous to each other and their customers. The store wouldn't donate to the benefit, but the managers allowed employees to sell tickets outside the door when they were off the clock.

Kim's a very interesting conversationalist. It's a conservative area, and Kim's politics aren't very conservative. She grew up in a fairly large city before moving out to the country with her husband. She's the Abbie Hoffman of Big Box.

Kim is good with money and manages to make ends meet, despite Big Box's seasonal cutbacks. She looks at the lost working hours as time she can spend with her grandchildren.

Madelyn and Gary met at Big Box eight years ago. They are in their late 20s and have two children together. They were married a year ago in a nearby park. They miraculously managed to take their vacations at the same time and had a three-day honeymoon in the northern part of the state.

Like many rural residents, Madelyn and Gary used to serve as firefighters in the local volunteer fire department. They have helped search for missing children and senior citizens who, suffering dementia, have wandered off. As emergency medical technicians, they have come to the aid of customers and coworkers countless times. But when they had their children, time constraints forced the two to give up their fire department membership. Madelyn works days; Gary works nights. That way, one of them is always home with their children.

Madelyn and Gary also live in a trailer park. They suspect their residence is the reason their daughter's teacher reported them for possible child abuse based on one small bruise on the girl's arm. After an investigation, the report was declared unfounded.

People in the community, including some Big Box customers, tend to make disparaging remarks about mobile-home residents. A teacher waiting in the checkout line talks about the range of quality in home schooling. Some home-schooled students are ahead of their peers in most subjects, she notes. "But you take a family in a trailer where the parent barely graduated high school and that child is learning nothing," she says. She reaches her turn in line and gives the cashier, me, a look as though I know nothing.

One Christmas, the store had a gingerbread-house decorating contest among workers. The winning gingerbread creation was a trailer home with a junk car sitting on concrete blocks in the front yard and a big blue tarpaulin covering the trailer's leaky roof.

Big Box workers have great senses of humor. They need to.

The head custodian, Willard, has perhaps the best sense of humor. Everyone likes him, and everyone relies on him. Though in his 30s, he lives with his parents, an eccentric couple known for ranting on a variety of topics. Willard is the only son. His three sisters don't have the patience to live with their parents.

"I make sure they take their pills," Willard says of the odd couple. He calls home every day at lunch to make sure the folks are OK.

He's had trouble finding a romantic partner. "When they hear I clean toilets at Big Box, they head for the hills," he says. If they make it past the Big Box obstacle, the bickering parents doom the relationship. Willard's sisters keep signing him up for online dating services, but he keeps sabotaging their computers. The last date they sent him to meet turned out to be a transvestite. The sisters had become a little confused when they wrote his profile, they explained to him. He'll find his own mate, thank you very much, sisters dear.

Herbert was a former nuclear physicist with a doctorate who spent years working abroad. He had become bored with retirement, so he took a job at Big Box for $8.40 an hour. He apparently also had become bored with his wife, a retired chemist from France, because he soon took up with Cassie, a former electrical engineer who had given up her career to be a stay-at-home mother. She came to Big Box to partially (very partially) offset some of the loss of her income. Herbert and Cassie resigned their Big Box jobs and became engaged. There was just one hitch. Herbert was still married and kept postponing the date he pledged to Cassie that he would be free. But Cassie was in love. She would wait and would bear whatever sacrifice was necessary. Her children no longer spoke to her.

And Inga had come to the United States with her husband shortly after World War II. They settled in the South, but found their neighbors resented German-speaking immigrants. Their house was firebombed. They moved north. Though Inga had hand-painted china in her native Bavaria, the local china maker refused to hire her. Her husband took good care of her, and she was happy to be a homemaker, she told me. But when he died suddenly, she was forced to go to work to make ends meet. Her husband had thought she could collect his Navy pension, but the Navy told her no. She was allowed to keep TRICARE, the military health insurance. She was 72. She had trouble seeing at night, but Big Box often scheduled her to work from 5 to 10 p.m., or sometimes to 11 p.m., and had her come in at 7 the next morning.

Maxine, though she had suffered several heart attacks, insisted on keeping her job. She also lived in a trailer park and had trouble making ends meet. After her last attack, she was out of work for several months. She returned wearing her cannula and toting her oxygen tank. At first, Maxine, who was 81, only was scheduled to answer the phone, so she could keep her tank on the desk. She folded clothes between calls. But soon the managers asked her to return to the floor. She could be seen hanging blouses in the ladies' section, her oxygen tank sitting beside her in a shopping cart, where most customers plopped their toddlers or their pocketbooks. Some of the other apparel workers worried that the store manager would tell her she couldn't use the shopping cart.

But there was precedent for employees using items designated for customers. When Emma fell off a ladder while stocking shelves and broke her leg, she was out of work only a few days. Longtime employees explained that the company had changed doctors it used for workers compensation cases when it learned one doctor believed in employees staying out of work until they were fully healed. Emma used a motorized shopping cart to get from aisle to aisle. Other employees teased her about her driving skills, since she sometimes bumped into the merchandise on the corners of the shelves.

Emma had to work. She and her husband, Earl, who had lost his job of 30 years when a local factory closed, had taken in their adult daughter, son-in-law and the couple's three children when the son-in-law was laid off from his job. "We'd do all right," Emma explained, "except we're supporting seven people." Earl had worked at Big Box for several years after the factory closed until his emphysema became so bad that he had to quit. His doctor had been urging him to quit for two years, but Earl was proud and wanted to keep working as long as possible. He was sent to my cash register to bag for me one busy Wednesday before Thanksgiving. I wondered why the usually jovial man seemed frustrated as he stuffed the bags. I later realized that he was struggling to breathe, and hiding it the best he could.

Emma was perpetually exhausted. Although her daughter, who still had a full-time job, cooked most of the meals, Emma was in charge of the cleanup. She also cared for her grandchildren while her daughter was working and her son-in-law was looking for work. Plus, much of the upkeep of their home fell to her, since Earl was no longer able to do it. Emma wasn't alone. Exhaustion was almost universal among Big Box workers.

But sadly, Emma was used to it. She had been working as a cashier for many years at many stores. Early in their marriage, Earl was in the military. Because the couple had to move often, Emma couldn't get a career established and ended up taking cashier work at whatever store was near the Army base.

When Willard's plantar fasciitis flared so badly that he couldn't do his work (foot, knee and back problems were common among workers, who suspected the problems were caused by the unforgiving concrete floors), he was assigned to sit in a wheelchair at the entrance and greet shoppers. Normally, workers would be fired for sitting on the job.

Most of the workers who were fired were full-time employees, although they often were scheduled to work only 34 hours a week, and had been with the company just shy of six years. Employees became vested in the company's profit-sharing plan at six years. My last year at Big Box, the company eliminated the profit-sharing plan, although it did increase its 401(k) match to a generous 6 percent of an employee's pay. Most employees couldn't afford to contribute to a 401(k). The rumor in the store was that management wanted to get rid of all full-time employees and replace them with part-timers, who were eligible for fewer health benefits.

College students, among the perennial part-timers, were in a unique position at Big Box. Theoretically, they would work part time until they earned a bachelor's or perhaps a master's degree, then they would leave to work in their chosen field. But the Great Recession prevented many of these graduates from finding jobs. Desperate for money to pay back student loans, they stayed at Big Box.

Amber is one of them. She graduated state college with a bachelor's degree in political science nearly a year ago. She lives with her parents, who still provide the bulk of her financial support. Although new federal law lets young people keep their parents' health insurance, Amber is eligible for Big Box health benefits. She can only afford a high-deductible plan that covers much less than her parents' family plan, but the law doesn't allow her to keep her parents' coverage if she's eligible for her own. "It's not fair," she says. Although she supports the health care reform of the Barack Obama administration, she worries about the effect on her parents, who will end up paying her high deductible if she becomes ill. An expansion of Medicare to cover all Americans would be simpler and more fair.

Amber does her work well, but she hasn't been tapped for a promotion. Her mother has convinced her to run for a seat on the town council, so she will have some intellectual outlet and will feel that she's contributing to society. Each year, the store asks employees to take a supposedly confidential survey. One of the questions is whether the work at Big Box constitutes a rewarding career. It would be laughable if it weren't pathetic.

Unlike Amber, some college students easily have received promotions to lower-level management positions, whether they were deserving of promotions or not. Some of these people managed to work their way up to salaried positions. Those who lacked competence simply forced their work on underlings while taking the credit. The nicknames for two such managers became "Dumb" and "Dumber." Of course, Dumb and Dumber made somewhere in the $40,000 a year range, while the average worker made about $22,000 a year. I learned these figures talking with sympathetic managers and my coworkers at lunch or during breaks.

Dumb and Dumber were fond of having workers put up a display one day, then making them tear it down and redo it the next. Meanwhile, the cutbacks meant the workers couldn't change the prices for items on the shelves when the company changed the prices in the store's computers. Prices changed often. During the week, when most of the food stamp clients shopped, they were lower. On the weekends, when the relatively more affluent shoppers came, they were higher.

When the prices didn't ring up right at the register, those customers who noticed balked. We cashiers would have to call a manager to confirm the price. While the manager ran to the other end of the store to check the price, the checkout lines grew long. The customers muttered and glared. Often, the customer had given up waiting and decided not to take the item by the time the manager returned. Some customers understood that the situation wasn't our fault, but others made rude comments. Some yelled. One once threw a can at a cashier, who ducked just in time to avoid being hit. When she yelled at the customer, she was disciplined.

And so it was into this world that I fell.

I was one of eight hires that September. Eight months later, there were two of us still working at Big Box. By the following September, I was the only one of my group left. I'd like to say the workers moved on to better jobs, but that wasn't always the case. Most of them simply couldn't put up with the job.

Routinely, only a small number of Big Box's hires would stay more than a few weeks. I was initially put to work on the floor, to do the most mind-numbing work I'd done since I had typed forms in a summer job when I was in college. I stuck it out for three months and asked a sympathetic manager to get me a cashier position. I would take a 20-cent-an-hour pay cut, but I just didn't see how I could stay otherwise. Being a cashier was far from a dream job, but it wasn't that bad.

Here's my story, mingled with Kim's, Madelyn and Gary's, Willard's, Herbert and Cassie's, Inga's, Maxine's, Emma and Earl's, Amber's and many others'.

⚑ Chapter 3

AUGUST

I went to work one sunny, pleasant August morning a few years after I'd begun work at Big Box thinking, as I always did, about how much the United States needs a living wage law -- not just a minimum wage. People work in the retail realm for a variety of reasons and whatever the reason, they deserve to be able to toil without worry about making ends meet.

As Gary said, "I don't want to be rich. I just want to get out of the (trailer) park, get a decent house, maybe get a decent car, so I can get rid of the old van." His children had been teasing their parents to adopt a dog from the local shelter, but, living in the trailer park, they had no yard for the dog. Even if they walked the dog several times a day, it just wasn't a good situation, Madelyn said. Plus, they weren't sure they could afford the vet bills, especially if the dog became ill.

Madelyn and Gary, and all the other Big Box workers, deserved to simply enjoy the summer morning as they strolled across the parking lot, leaving their vehicles to be damaged by runaway shopping carts.

The store where I worked is in picturesque lake country. The company was required to prepare an environmental impact study before the town would approve construction. The company concluded that the environment would not be negatively affected, and actually, would be enhanced, by the construction. I don't think anyone believed the company, but the store was built anyway.

To its credit, the company retained the natural lay of the land, preserving a small wetland area and trees that surround the site. Shoppers who drive along the town-maintained road that serves as the store's entrance have to stop in the spring to wait for a goose and her goslings to cross the road.

The sun sets beautifully at night over the hills and trees, and rises beautifully in the morning over more trees. Many nights, walking dog tired out of Big Box at the end of a shift, I would feel refreshed by the setting sun. I would be awed by the beauty, which contrasted with the ugly, boxy store and big paved parking lot. Nature does her best to work around Big Box.

And so do we people, putting on a friendly, smiling face for our customers, even as our backs ache, the skin on our hands cracks from dryness from touching so many surfaces so often and our knees lock into place from standing for hours at a time. We toil for less than a living wage, watching the prices go up on the items we ring out at the cash register and wondering how we might afford the higher prices. Yes, fortunately, some places offer better bargains than Big Box, but the years after the Great Recession were characterized by rising food and energy prices everywhere.

Our pay went up marginally during this time -- 40 cents

an hour annually for most people -- but it wasn't enough to keep up with rising costs. Many of my coworkers were on food stamps, had gone bankrupt, visited food pantries and church-run thrift stores regularly.

Big Box also got a great deal of its employees' business, mainly because the employees were already at the store, and if they needed something, they were too overworked and exhausted to make a trip elsewhere for it. It's lunchtime and you were too tired to pack a lunch? Try Big Box's deli, or a frozen meal from the grocery section. As a store greeter said to me one day when I rang out his purchases for his midshift meal, he could have bought a sit-down meal at a restaurant for what he paid for his takeout deli items.

But I digress.

This morning, I was in for a brief, welcome diversion. The clerk who was scheduled to work at the customer service counter had called in sick so she could take care of her daughter, who was recovering from surgery. Since the clerk was a rare full-time employee, she was eligible for sick pay -- but not for her first day of missed work. I was continually amazed at the bizarre rules the company came up with that, I thought, were designed to pinch pennies out of its work force. The first sick day was unpaid, or could be used as personal time or vacation time. The second sick day was paid -- if you were full time. If you were part time, as were most of the employees, no sick time was paid. Employees who took the allowed three sick days in a rolling six-month period were counseled by management not to take another sick day or they would be violating company policy. In other words, they would be on the road to being fired. Many parents of young children had lost their Big Box jobs this way. Toddlers just get sick too often. We need, I thought, mandatory, paid sick time -- and enough of it, especially for people in fields where they come into contact with the public's germs on a regular basis -- for every worker in the United States.

I came in at 8:30 that morning. Since 7 a.m., a low-level manager had been running register, tending to cashiers' requests for change and other needs, and rushing to the service counter every time a customer had a return, which was often at Big Box. Much of our merchandise was junk. Since I was trained in customer service, I spent my first hour and a half there, instead of running register. Cross training employees was popular, and a good idea from a staffing standpoint and the workers' standpoint, since it offered a little variety in an otherwise mostly monotonous day. But of course, it also meant employees often filled in at jobs that were a higher pay grade without ever getting the higher pay.

When I came from the sales floor to cashiering, the managers put through the paperwork for my 20-cent-an-hour pay cut right away. However, I continued to work on the sales floor for six weeks before I was switched to running register. Time and again, I heard employees tell of taking pay cuts when they changed jobs within the store or transferred from one store to another.

Most of my customers at the service desk that morning had returns. We also issued money orders and took utility payments at the desk. I was fluent in returns. In my time on the sales floor I had processed returns for the jewelry department. There were many returns. Once when I was showing a customer a pair of earrings, one of the earrings broke when I lifted it out of the showcase. Wisely, that customer passed up on the purchase. Many

17

customers didn't find out how fragile the merchandise was until they tried it on, usually at home, though a couple of customers returned watches minutes after buying them because they had fallen apart when the customers tried to take them out of the case to put them on before leaving the store.

It was in this way that I was conned by a thief. I was working alone at the jewelry counter when I got a rush of customers. I was putting a band on a customer's watch while a young couple looked at a showcase of rings. A man in a security guard uniform approached me to exchange a watch he had bought a few days earlier at another Big Box store. I temporarily left the watch band (one of the pins that would hold it to the watch wasn't cooperating anyway) to process his exchange. He left with the replacement watch. A few minutes later, just as I finished changing the watch band (I still had to ring the customer up for the band) and was preparing to show the couple diamond rings, while another customer waited to see a necklace, the security guard returned. He waited until I left the couple so the two could discuss the rings privately. "This watch broke when I was putting it on outside," he said. I wasn't surprised. He handed me the closed watch box. I should have opened the box, but his story sounded all too plausible, and I had four other customers waiting for my attention. I issued him a refund. About 30 minutes later, when the customers had cleared out, I opened the box. It held an obviously old, junk watch. The security guard had stolen a watch.

I felt bad. We employees always managed to take our work seriously, even if we sometimes doubted the managers took us seriously and even though we weren't paid much. We all wanted to do a good job. We wanted to do right by our customers and the company. I sometimes wondered why we cared so much, but care we did. Our employer made billions of dollars a year in profit while giving most of us subsistence wages, but we felt bad when we let a thief get away with a $13 watch.

Had I had help at the counter, I likely wouldn't have made that mistake. I stayed late to write out the details to leave for the store's loss prevention officer. Fortunately, I wasn't scheduled for 40 hours that week (I was almost never scheduled for 40 hours, even though I worked six days a week), so Big Box paid me the extra time I spent documenting the theft. If I had been at 40 hours, I would have been expected to take a longer lunch hour to make up the time. Employees who logged overtime were verbally warned. Repeated "offenses" resulted in termination. I was stubborn and refused to take a long lunch, so I came in as late as allowed and left as early as allowed to make up the time in those rare instances when I worked longer than scheduled in a 40-hour week.

All of the 40-hour weeks came in my first year of work, when I made a few cents less an hour than I did in subsequent years.

After I'd submitted the details of the theft, I learned on the company's database that the store didn't bother to prosecute thieves for minor thefts. The manager who directed me to document the details apparently had been misinformed.

Sadly, I also had learned, through experience, that many customers are nasty, rude, condescending or dismissive. Although we cashiers were instructed to cheerfully greet each customer, some customers ignored us throughout the transaction, never looking at our faces but maintaining an expression of disdain on theirs. One woman, as she picked up her filled bags, gave her cart a push into an aisle full of departing customers. I don't know if she noticed when I went to retrieve it.

I was used to encountering rude people from my work as a journalist. People either love reporters or hate them, and in my experience, people usually hate them. However, the sheer volume of customers at the store and the speed at which we were required to work meant I encountered many more obnoxious people during my four years at Big Box than I did in 21 years at newspapers. Sometimes it seemed that the condescending people were the worst. These were the people in professions or business or retired. We cashiers got the feeling that such customers assumed we were undereducated and, frankly, stupid. I doubt they realized how many of us had college degrees.

But to be fair, many customers were surprisingly pleasant. We so appreciated them. They made our day filled with greeting people, lifting, twisting, bagging and sorting much easier. One customer routinely would buy a doughnut from the in-store bakery to give to the greeter. I never was given a doughnut, but one summer day one of my regular customers brought me some pickles he had home canned. New cashiers routinely told me that the work experience made them pay better attention to how they treated retail employees. "I told my husband, 'You be nice to those cashiers. They have a hard job,'" one new cashier told me. "It's more physically tiring than you'd expect," I said. "And mentally exhausting," she observed. Another cashier compared our work to parenting a young child. "You're always talking and you're always moving," she said. You're also always trying to gauge the customer's wants. I never dreamed what strong feelings customers had about every aspect of bagging groceries, sundries and clothes until I came to Big Box. Of course, you can ask the customer his or her preferences, but it's impractical (and sometimes annoying to the customer) to ask a question on every bag.

We also learned that customers were more likely to be nice in the morning than at the end of their day. "We get all their frustrations," a coworker observed. I sometimes thought that we needed to be psychologists to run register. Actually, one cashier was studying to be a psychologist. I wondered if she could make a case for her time at Big Box as field experience?

I wondered if some of our customers had mood disorders. Some days they would be friendly; other days they were vile. One Christmas Eve, I had to get the store manager to calm down one often-friendly woman who suddenly threw a fit because the store had sold out of $25 American Express gift cards.

While some customers had us walking on eggshells, others left us inspired and speechless. The first time Bruce came through my line, I was shocked. I looked up to see a tall man unloading a cartful of groceries onto the conveyer belt using two clamps positioned at the end of long metal shafts. He had no forearms or hands. His arms above the rods appeared to be burned. His face was scarred, apparently from burns, and he couldn't speak above a whisper. He was alone; many customers who had disabilities shopped with a friend, relative or aide. I bagged his groceries and loaded them into his cart. He refused our carryout service. He carried his money in a zippered bank bag. He seemed to be growing tired, and so he asked me to put his change into the bag and zip it closed for him. The two women in line behind Bruce were silent. When he left, one said, "You don't know how lucky you have it..." She trailed off into silence again. The woman behind her nodded. In subsequent visits, Bruce would let me unload his cart for him and asked me to take the money out of his bag. But he never accepted help loading his vehicle.

Many of the customers who had disabilities used the local bus that stopped at the store once a week. Being a rural area, there was little public transportation available. We kept schedules of the sparse bus routes at the customer service desk. The only stop for shopping was Big Box, so customers were forced to buy their groceries, medicines and other goods there. Before Big Box was built, the bus stopped at a grocery store across the main highway and a department store up the road. Both stores closed soon after Big Box opened. Many people blamed Big Box for the closings, but the owners of those stores, interviewed by local media, cited declining sales long before Big Box came in. Big Box seemed to draw clientele that had previously traveled out of the immediate area for shopping. I wondered if the people who opposed Big Box's entry into the area had bothered to support the two local stores before Big Box was proposed. After Big Box opened, many of my neighbors who had spoken against the mega-retailer began shopping at it. A few of them were the customers who gave us cashiers condescending looks.

These were our customers that August morning. The morning went by relatively fast. Mornings usually went faster than afternoons, even though afternoons were busier. At first, being busy made the time go by fast. But after a few months, not even being busy helped. Though each customer and his or her groceries was different, giving us some variety, the job was boring. We also had little or no control over our work. If we had a moment of down time, managers put us to work on a task of their choosing. Sometimes we were lucky enough to find a sympathetic manager and suggest a task that wasn't as bad as one we were afraid would be given to us. I was reminded of how much, for many years, I had loved my work at newspapers, which was, ironically, the reason I left the newsroom. The years before and during the Great Recession were difficult for newspapers, which responded by paring staffs, cutting the amount of space allotted for news and often changing focus to less hard-hitting, lifestyle news. At least I had spent 21 years in a field I loved. I thought about how many young people were stuck at Big Box, college graduates unable to get work in the field of their choosing. What was the future for the youth of our country? What was the future of our country? The jobs, it seemed to me, had disappeared not because of changes in industries so much as the greed of a few.

It was like Kim said. Most of the world's problems came down to greed. Kim and I theorized that these changes would help: a living wage law, paid sick time, a rollout of the Medicare program to cover all Americans, including a component for dental care, and changes in Social Security to boost contributions of upper-income earners. But our ideas weren't popular among our mostly conservative comrades at Big Box. And Big Box workers were among those who would be helped by such measures. Kim and I discussed our theories the few times I gave her a ride home or when we were lucky enough to have lunch together. The company-generated schedules changed so much that we all had trouble keeping track. When someone inevitably got mixed up and came in at the wrong time or on the wrong day, the company put a note in the employee's file. Get too many notes and you'd be fired. Surprisingly, considering the speed at which many employees left, a solid number managed to work under these conditions and stay for years. Kim was among them. In five years, she had never taken a sick day or mixed up her constantly changing schedule.

Kim worried that she needed to see a doctor about her lungs. She often became short of breath and worried that it had to do with the fire she had survived a decade before. She had no health insurance and couldn't even afford Big Box's cheapest insurance plan. The cheap one, which I took, being healthy, cost $10 every two-week pay period. It was a high-deductible plan. The first $5,000 was paid out of pocket. I figured I could handle the deductible if necessary, because I had savings from my days working for a reasonable wage. Kim didn't have that luxury. Kim also was afraid that she needed more than a simple trip to the doctor -- likely lots of expensive tests because of the fire. She was afraid she made too much money to qualify for state-run insurance, but she planned to look into it. She also planned to check with a couple of clinics to see if she qualified for low-cost care.

Neither of us had dental insurance. As a part-timer, Kim wasn't eligible. Since I was full-time, I was eligible, but the insurance was more expensive than paying for a cleaning every six months or a year. As it was, I was stretching my cleanings to once every two years and fastidiously brushing and flossing. This scheme worked until my dentist retired. No independent dentist would take me without insurance, so I went to a dental group that catered to insuranceless people. Some of my coworkers at Big Box had gone there to get dentures and recommended the place. I got free X-rays. The cleaning and fluoride treatment were a reasonable price. But every six-month cleaning would include X-rays, which I couldn't afford and considered unnecessary and possibly dangerous. I figured the group made its money that way. I didn't plan to return for the six-month cleaning, but I wasn't sure what I would do.

Many of my coworkers had gone years without seeing a dentist. Most of them, and our customers, had missing teeth. Their remaining teeth were badly stained. Some of these people had atrocious breath. Emma's front tooth fell out. When she finally went to a dentist, the dentist told her she had advanced gingivitis because of going for many years without a routine cleaning. The dentist told her she was fortunate the bacteria hadn't harmed her health in other ways, contributing to heart, kidney or lung problems. Some employees managed to get dentures, usually through the group I had visited, or if the employee was enlisted with a military reserve, through the federal government. Many others struggled to chew their food with missing or bad teeth. I had never realized how necessary dental care was until I came to Big Box.

Kim and I finished our lunch. Kim, fortunately, had good teeth, as did I, at least for the time being. We had rested our aching feet for a while and were ready to go back to the front of the store and ring out customers, smiling as we packed bags, all the long afternoon.

We'd be exhausted by the time we left. We had a hard time explaining to people who didn't work at Big Box how draining the work was. If we had a busy night at the newspaper with breaking news or the general election -- the journalist's equivalent of Black Friday -- I would come home tired, but never like this. And I got paid so little to become so exhausted. I remembered a sociology professor when I was in college who said his wife, a social worker, used to complain that the people who collected her garbage were paid as much as she was. His reply had been, "How much money would it take to make you do that job?"

I thought of Willard, who had to clean bathrooms, sometimes cleaning diarrhea off the floor and toilet, or cleaning up vomit. He got paid less than we cashiers. I thought of the cashier who also worked as an aide at a hospital. The hospital custodians earned more than she did. They cleaned rooms after patients left, "but we're the ones who do the dirty work," my Big Box comrade said.

I thought about the babies who reached out with spit-covered hands for the rack that held my bags or gnawed on a frozen dinner that I had to touch. I thought about the toddlers, who, waiting with their parents in a long line, urinated in the carts, or the adults who licked their fingers to separate their bills as they paid in cash. Coins were less troublesome that way, although one customer pulled his change out of his pocket and handed me a quarter accompanied by a pubic hair. I also sometimes received change with dryer lint, which oddly I considered more disgusting than the pubic hair. Some customers also tried to be "helpful" and lick their fingers so they could open my plastic bags for me. Even when I assured them I could open the bags fast by myself, they insisted on "helping." Sometimes I could feel the spit on my arm when I loaded the groceries into the bag. We kept hand sanitizer at the register, but I never used it. The cashiers who did found it dried out their hands, which sometimes cracked painfully, giving germs an entry route into their bodies. I washed my hands as soon as I went on break. When I got home, I would wash up to my elbows and change my clothes. When Amber's niece was born, it would have been shorter for her to have gone directly to the hospital for a visit after work, but she refused to come near the baby without changing out of Big Box garb and showering first. I understood completely. I tried to avoid these bodily fluids as much as possible.

I rarely had to worry about these problems as a reporter. Sure, sometimes you would find yourself in a similar situation, but it wasn't routine like it was at Big Box. After the first few years in my chosen field, I was paid more than a cashier. When I started at Big Box, a few months before the Great Recession began, I was given maximum credit for having worked full time for 21 years and for having a four-year degree. I started at $9.80 an hour, high for routine retail work. Coworkers who also had four-year degrees and maximum work credits started for $8.40 an hour a year later, after the recession had set in. One cashier reminded me that I made more than many fast-food store managers. Several Big Box workers interviewed for management positions at local convenience stores, but found that they would be paid less than they made at Big Box, which, believe me, wasn't much when you were trying to live a modest but reasonably comfortable life. So much for the American dream. It was a myth anyway, Kim and I agreed.

Occasionally, I had customers who complained about "lazy" people not wanting work unless they were paid "big bucks." I wondered how much these customers would expect to be paid to do my job, or even if they would consider my work. One customer, a neighbor, told me it was good for me to do menial work. I had known this man most of my life. He had never had to do menial work, except for a laborer position he held during the summer months while he was in college. He resented local highway workers who earned $15 an hour or $16 an hour, which he thought was too much. Yet these workers plowed snow off highways hours upon hours with only a quick break for a meal during our harsh winters. They tarred roads in the unrelenting summer sun. He had gotten a job in his field directly out of college and had retired early to a generous pension. He had no idea what my situation was like or what the situation was for our young cashiers, recent college graduates saddled with debt from school who couldn't find a decent-paying job, let alone a job in their field. I had no patience with these people.

Another customer complained all through the time I rang up and bagged his groceries about his sad state of affairs. He had been laid off from a good job months before, he told me. He was collecting food stamps and unemployment benefits and just couldn't find another job. I felt sympathetic. "Where did you used to work?" I asked. He hesitated. "At the airport," he said. "What work did you do?" I asked. He hedged. I didn't press. He scanned his Electronic Benefits Transfer (EBT) card for his food purchases first. Then he had me put a few dollars on his debit card, which contained his unemployment benefits. He finished paying with his credit card. "Three cards to have to pay this," he said, shaking his head. "You know, it's gotten so bad that I just put in an application at Donut Delights (a chain doughnut shop). Me at Donut Delights. Can you imagine that?" He shook his head again. I gave him a blank expression and said nothing. Apparently, ringing up groceries in a low-pay job at

Big Box was good enough for me, but a low-pay job at Donut Delights was beneath him. What did he think my previous job had been? I no longer felt sympathetic toward him. I saw him a few times after that, checking out in Emma's line. It looked like he was complaining to her. Poor Emma.

Some of the cashiers resented our food stamp customers, though most of us didn't. The food stamp clients were among our most down-to-earth, friendly and appreciative customers. True, some were obnoxious, but that appeared to be the exception. I wondered if the strong strain of pride and independence that ran through our hardworking staff made some of them look poorly on those who needed a hand. Quite a few Big Box workers were on food stamps, especially the ones with children. A few of the cashiers made barely too much money to qualify for food stamps, even though they struggled financially. These especially seemed to be the ones -- who had been denied help themselves -- who resented those who had some aid. It was more than unfortunate that anyone needed food stamps. I was pleased when a customer would tell me she had just found a job and would be able to get off unemployment and food stamps. That was evidence that the program worked; it helped someone get back on her feet after a job loss. The last winter I worked at Big Box I received notice that, based on my previous year's income, I appeared to be eligible for the Home Energy Assistance Program, which helps the poor pay heating bills. Most people I talked to thought the program was designed for senior citizens, yet most of the people I knew who were eligible for the aid were working age, working at Big Box or another low-pay place. I didn't apply. I turned my thermostat down even more. I wore layers at home. My extended family members joked that they had to keep their coats on when they visited during the winter. One of my friends suggested that low wages created a culture of slave labor where workers resented each other for the tiny benefits one might get that the other was denied. In a culture of plenty, one person would have little reason to resent someone else for a few dollars a month in government aid. Big Box Stores Inc. consistently posted billions of dollars in profit a year. Surely it could afford to pay all of its workers a reasonable, living wage, enough to buy shelter, food, clothing, health care -- the necessities. A living wage was not too much to ask.

It was finally the end of my shift, and a good thing, because my patience was running out. I was relieved to walk across the long parking lot, admiring the surrounding trees this lovely day and get in my car, where I could be off my feet for the drive home. In the first few weeks I worked at Big Box, my feet hurt so much that I kept cork-soled sandals in my car so I could switch into them for the drive home. Big Box didn't allow workers to wear sandals, even though our feet sometimes swelled from standing on them for hours at a time. I enjoyed the drive home. I took my pleasure where I could. If my work no longer satisfied me, I would derive extra pleasure from the simple things -- a gentle breeze, a beautiful sunset, the smell of freshly mown grass coming from the lawns of houses I passed on the way to my own modest, but comfortable home.

Once home, like my coworkers, I was too exhausted to want to cook dinner. When I'd made a living wage, popping a frozen dinner in the microwave oven hadn't been such a terrible idea. But on my budget, I wondered if I could afford such luxuries. It was a Catch-22. We cashiers were too exhausted to prepare meals from scratch but too poor not to. More often than I cared to admit, I gave in to the frozen dinner and pinched my budget elsewhere. But as the years dragged on at Big Box and I became increasing worried about my ability to make ends meet without draining my savings, I increasingly found myself making poor food choices. I would eat a big bag of salty potato chips, then pay later when my feet swelled and hurt. Sometimes I had a sandwich, which wasn't a bad choice. I reminded myself that I'd cost myself a lot more money if my health deteriorated. But what did people do who really couldn't afford good food? Some of my customers told me they received about $30 a month in food stamps for two people. Food pantries couldn't possibly fill all the need that I was becoming aware was out there. But regardless, I was always ravenous by dinnertime -- whenever that turned out to be. Big Box's shifts were constantly changing.

The constantly changing mealtimes were especially hard on the workers who were diabetic -- and there seemed to be a lot of them. I wondered if the stress, fatigue and generally bizarre schedules brought on diabetes in those already prone to the disease. Madelyn told me her doctor had advised her to develop set mealtimes to help control her blood sugar levels and thereby delay or prevent the complications of her disease. Diabetics can suffer blindness, heart and kidney disease and amputations. She said to her doctor, "Do you know where I work?"

Another worker was having tests (she had health insurance through her husband's employer) to determine whether she was in the beginning stages of heart disease. Her doctor told her to avoid strenuous work. He knew she was a cashier, but he told her she should continue working. Apparently he couldn't fathom how repeatedly lifting 24-packs of water bottles and 40-pound bags of cat litter could be strenuous to a woman who had most likely had a heart attack days before. I told her she should see a different cardiologist. Her insurance allowed a second opinion, but she couldn't afford the $40 co-pay. And of course, getting Big Box to arrange her work schedule so she could take the tests was a challenge. When I worked as a professional, I had the flexibility to adjust my schedule, within reason, around outside responsibilities. I had especially valued this perk, though I somehow didn't see it as a perk, when I was caring for my sick mother in the final years of her life. But in the low-wage world, there was little flexibility. If you were lucky, you could find a sympathetic manager. But to many of the managers, you were just some warm body who punched a time clock and obeyed orders.

As I stood at the register in the few moments between customers one weekday morning when the store wasn't too busy, I looked at a back-to-school display. A large cardboard crayon held teachers' lists of school supplies they required to be bought by their students' parents (or grandparents -- I noticed a significant number of grandparents, including Emma, were paying for their grandchildren's school supplies, probably because the parents couldn't afford them). How creative, I thought, admiring the display. I knew from writing stories and headlines that creativity takes time. You need a few moments to come up with a cute display or a catchy phrase. But we were barely allowed a breath between customers and we were seldom allowed to create a display, unless perhaps it was of clearance items. Mostly, we were treated like machines. More than one cashier described the work as degrading. True to form, a manager happened to walk by just as I was looking at the "crayon" display and keeping an eye out for customers who looked as though they might be ready to check out. The manager ordered me to neaten the nearby shelves.

One rare morning I was allowed to attend the meeting where the managers discussed sales figures and upcoming merchandise promotions. We cashiers were rarely allowed to attend the meetings because we were expected to constantly ring out customers, clean conveyor belts, tidy the register drawer or neaten the shelves. I was thrilled to have a moment when I could just listen to someone without having to constantly be in motion. The manager was directing the low-level managers at the meeting to leave notes for their overnight crews with detailed explanations of work to be completed. "You might tell them to zone the grocery shelves," he said. Zone, I had learned, meant to neaten. "But you might know that aisle 3 is a mess. They might work on aisles 1 and 2 and never zone aisle 3. They don't know that aisle 3 needs work unless you tell them." I wondered if he thought his overnight workers were stupid. He honestly thought that these people couldn't tell which aisles were the least tidy. If aisle 3 didn't get "zoned," I could tell him the probable reasons why. Most likely, in the six hours between the time the low-level manager left and the overnight crew had come in, the customers, during the store's busy on-the-way-home-from-work-let's-stop-at-the-store time, had made a bigger mess of aisles 1 and 2. Or perhaps the night crew had been busy doing some other work thrust on the workers by the night manager, such as unloading a truck. Or perhaps the night crew had had to clean up the coffee dribbled through the aisles by a customer, direct customers to merchandise, answer customers' questions, process returns or deal with any other problems that could have risen during the short-staffed hours between 10 p.m. and 7 a.m. The lack of respect was frustrating. The manager's rank and pay apparently made him consider himself smarter than his underlings. I thought about unions that had fought to get good pay for people who toiled in dirty, noisy factories. One neighbor had retired from General Motors. Her pension and Social Security income equalled my take home pay during my top-earning years at the newspaper. She was smart enough, but she was a high school dropout who had never had trouble getting a job. I was a college graduate with a bachelor's degree and 21 years of full-time work experience who couldn't find a living wage job. I worried, once again, about the recent college graduates, such as Amber, who were stuck at the store because they couldn't find jobs in their fields. Would they ever find jobs in their fields? My cousin, who worked for a development company, told me his firm had advertised for a $9-an-hour receptionist job and received 20 applications from people who had master's degrees. What about people like me, displaced middle-aged professionals, too young to retire but too old to be considered by most employers?

If we had a single-payer, government-run and government-paid health-care system, employers might not be so quick to overlook experienced, older workers. Big Box actually had a good record for hiring older workers -- I had to give the company credit for that.

Emma suggested we needed mental health days (we were lucky if we got sick days) in our line of work. Better pay and a little more time off would have helped wonders. Remember, to make ends meet, I had to work six days a week. If the company would schedule people to work 40 hours in five days, it would have helped tremendously. And the constantly changing days off meant some of us worked 21 days straight. It was exhausting, as the cashiers said, both physically and mentally.

And soon, we would have the back-to-school crowd to wait on. Although some local school district employees had worked during the summer, many had taken the two months between the end of one school year and the start of the next as an extended vacation. These people often complained to us cashiers about having to go back to work. We cashiers would have been glad to have had just two weeks of vacation, say nothing about two months, plus all the time off during the school year. Many of these workers made good, professional-level pay (their salaries are public information). But many made about what we cashiers made, even though they might have a master's degree and teaching certification, working as aides. The school districts reminded me of Big Box in their pay differences. If everyone were paid a decent wage, the top earners a little less and the bottom earners a lot more, the districts could educate students for the same amount of money while becoming the model of a more egalitarian system. I was probably too idealistic. One teachers aide, who had kept her part-time Big Box job that she got when she started college, complained that she did more work educating her students for $22,000 a year, despite having a master's degree and teaching certification, than the teachers did for $70,000 a year. Watching this woman work, interacting with other employees, I believed her. It wasn't just the retail world that needed a pay and policy revamp. It really seemed to extend across many fields, this inequality in pay and benefits. Anyone who said the difference was based on education or experience wasn't looking at the workers who were ringing out customers, folding clothes, stocking shelves or sweeping the floors.

This morning we were treated to some of my favorite customers -- migrant farmworkers. These young men, though they often spoke little English, were unfailingly polite. They came in once every few weeks to get groceries during the summer harvest. They bought rice and beans, pork chops and chicken, tomatoes and jalapenos. The food they bought was healthier than the food many of the customers bought. Because they were buying for their encampment, their orders were huge. Sometimes we'd team up to cash them out, one cashier ringing out the items and another bagging the food. The men came in groups of three or four, brought by the farmer, who waited patiently as they went through the line. I was grateful to these young men who labored in the fields, also for little pay, less than I earned at Big Box, picking the produce that I and others would eat in a few days. In this rural area, we had a culture of appreciating the farmer, but we often ignored the farmhands.

I was sure these farmworkers didn't have health insurance. Though I and some of my coworkers did, through Big Box, our high-deductible plan in effect meant we couldn't afford to go to the doctor. I kept my cheap insurance -- you couldn't beat $20 a month -- in case something catastrophic happened and I found myself with huge medical bills or in case I was fortunate enough to become pregnant late in life. My insurance would save me then. But realistically, I couldn't go to the doctor if I just plain got sick. And the sick day policy meant most of the workers couldn't afford to take time off for illness. A local restaurant had an outbreak of the flu during the time I was at Big Box. Not only were the restaurant's workers ill, but many of the customers became ill, as well. The local health department suspected that sick workers, who couldn't afford to take time off, had spread the flu to the rest of the staff and the customers. The restaurant was closed for a thorough cleaning. If workers were guaranteed paid sick time, the problem never would have happened. To add to the problem at Big Box, if a worker were out three days -- say for the flu, and we were constantly exposed to germs from the customers -- the worker needed a doctor's note to return to work. But of course, the worker couldn't afford to go to the doctor. This situation meant people routinely worked when they were ill. This meant they further exposed their coworkers and customers to colds and the flu.

The clerks at the customer service desk often refunded customers for deli purchases. "I can't tell you how many times customers have come to me and said, 'The woman at the deli was coughing so much when she got my order that I just can't bring myself to eat this,'" one of the clerks told me. One winter, cases of the flu became so numerous that workers would be forced to grab the nearest trash can so they could throw up. We workers felt bad for one such cashier, who, clinging to a trash bin, had to leave her register in the middle of a transaction. A low-level manager came to finish ringing out the customer. A sign soon appeared at the time clock, "If you are ill, please clock in and discuss the situation with a manager."

We sometimes got such signs, which were never helpful. "Wash hands with soap and warm water," one by the sink read. It never mentioned how long one should wash one's hands (20 seconds, I had learned when I was a volunteer at the local hospice). The company never invested in signs for our registers that would direct customers to keep heavy items in their cart, even though I and other cashiers repeatedly asked for them. The managers unfailingly told us it was a great idea, but in 14 months of asking, we never got the signs. Meanwhile, our backs ached and the tendonitis in our wrists flared. And we couldn't afford to go to the doctor. I took more aspirin in the four years I worked at Big Box than I'd probably taken in 40 years. I finally gave up and went to my chiropractor. Chiropractic care wasn't covered under my Big Box insurance, even if I had met the $5,000 deductible. My chiropractor mercilessly charged much less than a primary care physician, $34 per visit. If Big Box had encouraged chiropractic care, employees could have alleviated much of their discomfort for much less than the cost of visiting a primary care doctor or specialist.

Our insurance didn't cover any injury that came about during participation in a "riot or insurrection," according to the 2008 employee benefits handbook. I wondered how easily the company could consider a peaceful free speech protest that got out of hand a "riot or insurrection." Neither would the plan cover "charges occurred directly or indirectly while under the influence of illegal drugs." It would not cover abortions, even though they were legal in the state, "except when the health of the mother would be in danger if the fetus were carried to term, the fetus could not survive the birthing process, or death would be imminent after birth." Rape, including incest, was never mentioned, although perhaps a doctor could try to make a case for abortion under the "health of the mother" clause.

Much to my surprise, many people whom I told about these restrictions thought they were fine. Though I didn't expect to need care for substance abuse (which was covered under certain circumstances) or an abortion, I thought that I should have a legal right to have those services paid. In the case of abortion, the company was forcing its political views on its employees. Sadly, the company was not alone in making such restrictions. Workers employed by local churches couldn't get abortions paid through their health insurance. The first fall I worked at Big Box, the company was criticized in the media for sending an email to managers with an obvious message: vote Republican in national elections. One of the local managers confirmed getting the email. The manager planned to vote Democratic. The email had only confirmed the manager's decision.

Politics came up in interesting ways. One worker whose spouse was transgender told me about being called in to the office and told not to discuss personal issues with other employees. She was making other employees uncomfortable by mentioning her transgender spouse and referring to her spouse using the feminine pronoun, the manager said. I knew of no employees who were uncomfortable, although I did hear a few refer to the spouse as "it," a fact that the employee said had convinced her spouse to stop shopping at the store. The employee reverted to referring to her spouse as her husband. She was soon fired for leaving early one day when ill. The managers had had to call an ambulance for her, but they wouldn't consider her leaving an approved absence. She was consulting a lawyer, who was preparing a suit against the company. I wished that she would bring the transgender issue up; I considered it a clear case of discrimination. But her lawyer felt she should address the firing over a health issue. It was a sad situation. It was the 21st century, and this large retailer was behind the times.

Was the company aware of how many of its customers at the jewelry counter were members of the gay, lesbian, bisexual and transgender community?

Back at the register, I was lifting cases of water again. Why on earth did people buy so much bottled water? Emma suggested I tell my customers, after I'd scanned the water, "This is all set for you to take," and leave it for the customer to lift. "You chump, you put it up there, you take if off," was her theory. Sometimes it worked, but sometimes the customers just expected you to lift it for them (full-service, you know) and sometimes I just felt guilty if I didn't lift it. One or two wasn't bad to lift, but lift dozens in a day, and it could give your tendonitis reason to flare up.

Mercifully, lunchtime came soon. I joined Willard in the employee lounge at the back of the store. It was a windowless room, but midway through my tenure, the store manager invested in satellite television, so we could watch the news, crime drama reruns and soap operas. Willard was having a variation of beef stroganoff he'd come up with using white button mushrooms and the stems from portobellos instead of beef. He had started culinary school years before, but after spending a summer helping a friend at a catering business, he had decided the work wasn't for him. The long hours bothered him. Frankly, I couldn't imagine how cleaning toilets could be preferable to catering parties, but it was his decision. Willard found a creative outlet in cooking for his family. His sister was vegan, but his parents loved meat. Willard was often adjusting recipes so he could satisfy his diverse family. He also loved telling tales about his relatives, who sounded like an eccentric, but lovable, hilarious bunch. Willard was a great storyteller. The state fair was coming up and Willard told me he was relieved that his cousins from Arkansas weren't visiting. "Don't get me wrong; I love them," he said. Then he continued with his story. Last year, his cousin, who could make duck calls without using a call, had interrupted the duck calling contest. It took the judges a while to figure out that the cousin, who was in the audience, was the source of the strangely realistic calls that were coming from outside the arena. Willard arrived just in time to see the fair staff escorting his cousins out of the building. Being loyal and protective, Willard balked. "These people aren't doing anything. Why are you asking them to leave?" he said. "They're disturbing the contest," the staff member said. Willard wouldn't back down. A police officer was called to escort Willard and the cousins away. It wasn't until they reached the parking lot that the cousins told Willard, "You know, Cousin Joe can do a duck call without a call…" "And why didn't you tell me this before the police came?" Willard asked. Lunch was almost over and Willard left to call his parents, to make sure they were OK and didn't need anything.

I wondered about all the talent that was stifled at Big Box. Sometimes, if there was old merchandise that needed to be put on clearance sale, the clerks would be allowed to design and set up a display themselves. But most often, they had to execute a plan that someone else had designed. The clerks told me that they found some satisfaction, as well as frustration, in doing a display based on someone else's design because these displays often didn't come together according to plan. The clerks would have to improvise. They genuinely wanted the merchandise to look good and the customers to have the information, such as pricing, that the customers needed to make an informed purchase. They cared about their work. But they had to seek out these little moments when they could use their creativity. If each clerk could design and set up her (or his, but usually her) own displays, perhaps with help from a more experienced clerk, she could derive a lot more job satisfaction, I thought. Instead, I sometimes felt that we were treated like machines. We weren't allowed independence or autonomy or trust.

Trust was a big issue. I was offended when I learned that the receipt for each return or exchange had to be initialed by a manager for fear we cashiers and clerks would steal the merchandise. Yet we had been required to undergo criminal background checks before we were hired. Often, when a manager or clerk was fired, the rumor would spread that the person had been caught stealing. We never knew who started these rumors, which never seemed to fit the impression we had of the fired employee. One such employee, who had been refused access to the store tapes that supposedly showed her stealing merchandise, was consulting a lawyer about a possible lawsuit. I wondered how she could afford a lawyer, but she said her parents had offered to help her financially. She hadn't been charged, but she was deeply offended by the accusation and wanted her name cleared. I wondered how far she would get against a large retailer. The woman had worked at Big Box for five years and had an exemplary record. Nothing in her situation had changed, except that she had accumulated five years of yearly 40-cent-an-hour pay raises, so what would cause her to suddenly become a thief? We also noticed that many such "thieves" were full-time employees.

Sometimes, someone who had been able to put up with the monotony and degrading aspects of the work for years would reach a point where it was just too much to deal with any longer. For me, that point came one Sunday morning when I was asked to stuff advertising and preprint news sections into the newspaper that I had formerly written for, designed pages for, and edited. I left with the hope of never returning. The store manager, who I think was relieved to be rid of another full-time employee, noted on my termination paperwork that I was eligible to be rehired. They had never had a problem with me, she said. I wondered how I had been able to hold my tongue for four years.

Emma had had a different experience. Her years of cashiering at Big Box and other stores finally got to her one afternoon. There weren't many customers. It was October, one of the slow months for retailers when the summer tourists and campers were gone and the back-to-school sales had passed. She had been sent to fold clothes in the women's section. She had folded clothes for three hours straight. Big Box gave employees breaks every 90 minutes to three hours at the store's convenience. Years before, the company had fallen into a habit of forgetting breaks or directing employees to perform other work during their "breaks." Employees in our state had brought a class action suit against the retailer, which was settled out of court with affected employees receiving cash settlements. I got a little more than $100. The company had mostly cleaned up its act with regard to breaks by the time I was hired. I had experienced a few missed breaks. Others, who had worked at Big Box longer than I had, told me they received about $300. Sadly, several employees, for fear the company would retaliate against them, wouldn't join the suit even though they had been denied many breaks.

So Emma was coming to her break time. She was trying to hang on. But she thought about how many years she had been a cashier and how, at many points during those years, customers would be so impressed by the care she took helping them that they would seek out a manager to compliment Emma. If a customer had disabilities, Emma went out of her way to help. She would unload the customer's cart, check with the customer to make sure she wasn't making the bags too heavy, reload the cart and call for carryout service early enough that the helper would arrive just as the customer was ready to leave. Customers hated waiting for the carryout service. They didn't realize or didn't care that the people doing the carryout were usually outside trying to corral carts that had been left around the parking lot. It took some time to put the carts you were pushing in the appropriate place and get inside to the register. Emma always took care of her customers. Yet here she was, folding clothes, away from the customers whom she served so well. And just this morning, ignoring her years of exemplary service, a manager had complained because one of her customers had forgotten to take one of his bags. "Do you know that customer had to drive five miles back here to get that item?" the manager barked. "I know," Emma had said. "And I usually double check to make sure my customers have all their bags, but this morning I guess I forgot to do that with this one gentleman. I guess I was just so tired." "That's no excuse," the manager said. A few minutes later, Emma was sent to fold clothes.

Cashiers spent on average two to three minutes with each customer and scanned upwards of 400 items per minute. When you were ringing up customers, you were constantly in motion, scanning, bagging, scanning, bagging. And you had to make sure you bagged items according to category; cold and frozen items didn't go with hot food from the delicatessen. Chemicals didn't go with food. Clothes went in bags separate from food, toiletries or chemicals. Some customers sorted their items as they placed them on the conveyor belt. Others didn't. Some customers thought cashiering was mindless work. It was monotonous work, but it wasn't mindless. The good thing about this monotony compared with the monotony on the sales floor was that the items you scanned were different with each customer. But we saw so many customers that we usually couldn't remember what we had put in the last bag or sometimes even what our current customer looked like. Customers never needed to fear for their privacy with us, because we could never remember what they bought. Some customers remarked that we should be able to give them their change without looking at the display on the cash register. Certainly, we could add and subtract (I think some customers thought we couldn't), but there were so many customers in such a short time that we would forget the merchandise total by the time the cash drawer opened. Yes, Emma was tired.

Emma just couldn't stand it. She walked away. In the back of the store, she found the store manager. She quit. The manager told her she wouldn't be eligible to be rehired because she had left on short notice. By the following week, Emma was regretting her decision. It wasn't a good job and it was exhausting, but the job market was bad and her family needed the small amount of income the job provided. She contacted the store manager, who relented and let her return. However, she would take a 40-cent-an-hour pay cut. Many other employees told me they had transferred among stores within the company or had transferred jobs within the same store and had been required to take pay cuts. I was sure that had I wanted to return, I would have started at a much lower pay rate than I began at four years earlier.

Emma held her tongue and muddled through, as did we all. I often wondered how the people on the floor could stand the work folding clothes and stocking shelves according to someone else's plan. For sure, employees sometimes vented to each other in the lounge. I remembered how I had listened to police officers vent their frustrations to each other when, as a young reporter, I had been assigned to visit police stations and look through logs of calls and arrests. When a job is stressful, employees often rely on each other for support.

I saw such support often at Big Box. Workers who couldn't get time off for a doctor's appointment (if they could afford to visit the doctor) or a family obligation would look to their coworkers to switch shifts with them. We were required to have all time off requests in the computer system three weeks in advance. Often, it wasn't realistic. Even if we could get the request in early, it usually wasn't granted until just before the schedule came out. There was very little flexibility. If we could find a manager, the manager would often tell us to "just put the date in the system." And finding a manager was difficult, since we weren't allowed to leave our registers without permission, even to use the restroom, and we certainly couldn't flag down a manager when we had a long line of customers awaiting our services. If there wasn't time to enter the date three weeks in advance, the manager would tell us to find someone to take the shift. Again, I felt like were we seen as machines rather than people with lives and responsibilities. One's child did not necessarily give warning three weeks in advance of needing to see a specialist.

We were frustrated. The frustration and lack of control over our schedules or our work contributed to the stress and exhaustion we felt each day. People thought working under five deadlines a night as a newspaper editor was stressful. It was a cake walk compared with this.

Maxine needed to have a cataract removed. She had just had one removed from her left eye, having booked the surgery far enough in advance to satisfy the store's scheduling requirements. The doctor wanted her to have the right eye operated on the following week. "It's too soon! I can't get the time off!" she told the doctor. Her insurance required her to have the second surgery within a month or she would have to retake her preoperative tests. The store schedule hadn't been posted for the last day available to her to have the surgery. She asked a manager for the time off. "I'm going to need that shift filled," he said. "Get someone to cover it." Emma, though she hated folding clothes and tidying the women's section, where Maxine worked, volunteered to take the shift.

"No," Maxine said. "The schedule isn't done yet. They're just going to have to fill it." She again made her case to the manager. Apparently, this time he listened to everything she said. He filled the shift and gave Maxine the day off, as well as several days after the surgery. Maxine wondered aloud if she had come close to be disciplined for her audacity.

THE HOLIDAYS COMETH

It was October and beautiful in the countryside surrounding the store. A northern state, we were blessed with glorious fall foliage. Our soft maples turned fiery red and our hard maples glistened brilliant yellow after a rainfall. There were oranges and greens and golds and purples among the plant life. The days grew short. The football season at the local high school was in full swing. I enjoyed seeing the students come in after a game, some of them, especially the cheerleaders, still in uniform. There were fall festivals galore. We had some leaf-peeping tourists, and Halloween was a busy day. But mostly it was a month when days were slow. The store cut back on hours and the employees who could afford the cuts got a chance to have a small amount of time off. But increasingly, as the economy remained weak, employees had to sign up for any shift they could find.

That was how I signed up for a cart pusher shift. Not being adept at directing a stack of more than three carts at a time, I was relieved when my coworkers, two strong young men, suggested I collect the stragglers from the parking lot. The managers had been skeptical that a 47-year-old woman who usually wore skirts to work could handle a shift with the carts. Granted, I didn't wear a skirt that day. Jeans were allowed for cart pushers, back room help and custodians. The rest of us had to wear dark shirts and tan bottoms. When I saw a coworker shortly after I left Big Box, he joked that I had probably burned all my navy and khaki. I hadn't, though I never wore it. I wondered if, among the right crowd, it would make a really scary Halloween costume. So mostly, that glorious fall day I spent in the parking lot taking carts after customers using the handicapped parking spaces were finished with them. It was a dry, comfortable, beautiful day and I welcomed the chance to be outside, away from the managers and even away from most of the customers. But the cart pushers, who were paid less than we cashiers, had a hard job. They worked in rain, snow, sleet and blistering heat. They also provided carryout service, and if they couldn't get inside right away to help a customer, they heard complaints. If a customer's car got a tiny dent from a cart, they heard about it. They occasionally had to jump out of the way when a careless driver ignored them in their fluorescent vests and nearly ran them down. I'm proud to say that the day I worked the carts, the store manager toured the lot and complimented us on how good the area looked, free of trash and stray carts. We almost never received a compliment. As I told the lower-level managers, who were as surprised as we cart pushers were to get praise, it was the men who had done the vast majority of the work. But my attention to the stray carts had made a difference, I was told. And it was true. If the store would routinely staff the lot with just one more person, the lot would look better, the customers' cars wouldn't be hit by runaway carts and the carryout service would run faster. Some people told me that customers didn't expect good service when they paid bargain prices, but that wasn't my experience. And frankly, the customers had a right to expect good service. The only people receiving low pay for working at a discount store were the rank-and-file workers. The managers earned reasonable pay. The children of the company founders were billionaires. There was plenty of profit to be made at a discount store; the profit just didn't go to the people who did the hardest, dirtiest, most thankless work. After that day, if I had time and didn't have a line of customers, I tried to do at least a few of the carryouts myself for my customers, unless they had something really bulky or heavy to load. It was good to do something different, and it felt really good to have the freedom to decide to shut off the light at my register, signaling my unavailability, and perform another task. Self-direction was scare, and I longed for the freedom to decide my own fate. Sometimes, if it was slow and we had a sympathetic manager around, we even dared shut off our light, tell our neighboring cashier that we were running to the restroom, and have the chance to leave the register for a minute or two without asking permission or getting paged over the intercom system.

November came and we were getting ready for Thanksgiving and the Black Friday rush. We also had to prepare for the hunters. We did a fairly good business in camouflage clothing, doe estrus, ammunition, targets, hunting licenses, bows, tree stands, arrows and generally most things related to small- and big-game hunting, not to mention fishing, which seemed to know no season. From trout season in the spring through ice fishing in the winter, we sold kerosene lamps, fishing poles, lures, and of course, fishing licenses. Some of our customers wore waders into the store. We were busy.

I sometimes wondered if an irate customer, or even an employee, would come in some day with a machine gun and open fire. Fortunately, at least while I worked at the store, the only act of violence we witnessed was a disturbed soldier, newly back from serving in Iraq, who tried to strangle his wife in the ladies' room one Thanksgiving. A manager, who was later fired for supposedly stealing, intervened, subduing the man until police arrived. The wife escaped physically unharmed. Among the employees, there was sympathy for both the wife and the soldier. Many young people in the area enlisted in the military. "Really, the military should have given the soldier some counseling coming back from over there," the employees said. "He was in the wrong, but you can't entirely blame him."

We had another domestic case in which blows were nearly exchanged. An ex-boyfriend followed a woman and her neighbor, who happened to be a man, into the store. The jealous ex-boyfriend tried to pick a fight with the neighbor, but left when a manager approached. Another employee watched to make sure that the ex-boyfriend didn't wait in the parking lot and follow the other two when they left. By and large, the employees watched out for their customers and each other. Their kindnesses helped make the job bearable.

In the early days of the store, which had been open five years when I started work, managers and non-managers alike helped each other, talked and listened to each other and tried their best to be flexible. I heard these reports from the longterm workers at the store. Retail work sees a high turnover, and it seemed that our store had a high turnover, but the store manager pointed out in a meeting that half the store's employees had been at the store since its first year of operation. Such low turnover was rare, and a source of pride for the store manager. But the flexibility, and the relatively higher pay, thanks to quarterly bonuses in the hundreds of dollars, which had dwindled and then disappeared when I was working there, had been much of the reason for the store's success in retaining employees and probably, in generating sales. Did the company really save by cutting back on its staff? Our sales were falling. Morale was falling. Employees who could transfer to other, more profitable stores, or could find better jobs, did. These were longterm employees, who knew the job the best and could be of the most help to customers. We were left with a less-experienced staff. Employees who could get management positions did, whether they were ready to be good managers or not. But many employees were just stuck at Big Box. The job market was bleak, even though the Great Recession had officially ended two years before.

Thanksgiving was actually fun my first couple of years at the store. Customers and employees alike were anticipating the holiday season. Our customers mostly seemed jovial before Thanksgiving. After about 7 a.m. on Black Friday was another situation entirely. The phrase "holiday spirit" took on a whole new, sinister meaning when I came to Big Box. We learned that Christmas truly brings out the worst in tired, frustrated, financially stressed shoppers. "'Tis the season!" we'd say sarcastically to each other as we workers passed in the aisles.

But Thanksgiving was our calm before the storm. Customers were patient, even though they might wait in lines that snaked down "action alley," the main aisle of the store. In the first years, we had enough employees so that people came from the sales floor and the loading dock to bag for us cashiers on the day before Thanksgiving, when we had lines of customers past the cash registers and well into the aisles. In the week before Thanksgiving, the heavy frozen turkeys would hit the bottom of the bags with a thud, but the customers never complained. They might even crack a joke. Other times, they would complain about us "dropping" their food. I so wanted to let loose with a tirade on one particularly obnoxious such customer late one day, but I held my tongue. I think the customers realized that we couldn't speak our minds. They took advantage of that fact and were mean. We always had to hold our tongues. All I could do was glare at the customer, and glare I did, for sure.

But Thanksgiving was different. Black Friday, even, was good. We came in early and mostly our customers were happy. By about 7 a.m., when they had been up 24 hours, customers started to get cranky. But mostly, early in the day, it was a jovial, almost carnival atmosphere. Some customers wore Santa hats and dressed in red and green. The first couple of years, we were allowed to dress up for the occasion. In later years, after a death during a Black Friday rush at a store, we had to remain dressed in our company colors as part of a safety plan. Apparently, the store wanted us easily recognizable as employees. True, we did often have to flash our name badges to get through the lines outside the entrance on Black Friday morning before the store opened. Dressed in our Big Box garb, the customers easily recognized us. No one else would wear such ugly colors.

Before long, we would be getting snow, which would add to the holiday spirit, until the holiday spirit showed its more sinister side. One snowless day, a middle-aged woman came through my line and looked at me differently than most of my customers. She looked as though she was soldier meeting a fellow soldier. "I worked for Big Box back when Dean (Bliven, the company founder) was still alive," she said. "It was different then. Dean was sick and the company was just beginning to act like a corporation. Already, there were some changes. I don't think Dean was aware of them. I didn't stay long. It's a hard job. People don't realized how hard it is." I heard such observations whenever I encountered someone who had worked for Big Box in the years when its founder was in charge. "Dean treated his employees like family," these former workers would say. "He would never put up with the way they treat workers now." It was interesting, because I had read about Big Box being evil from the start, discriminating against women and minorities. These people had a different view. I wondered what Dean Bliven would have thought of the 21st century Big Box.

Sometimes, I got a sense that some contemporary stores might still be somewhat family-like, if that was how all stores had been in the beginning. Employees from stores in the south, where Big Box began, would go through my line and proudly tell me which store they worked in. They greeted me as a friend. Company truck drivers greeted me similarly. They sounded as though they enjoyed their work. The truck drivers were paid considerably more than the sales floor staff, so that may have figured into their attitude. It was easier to be cheerful when you didn't have to worry whether you would get enough hours to pay the bills this month. It was easier to be cheerful when you didn't have to work two jobs and work six days a week. It was easier to be cheerful when you weren't supporting, not only your own nuclear family, but your grandchildren or your parent, as well. It was easier to be cheerful when you weren't exhausted. I had to wonder how the fatigue and worry affected everyone's health.

Kim had a great attitude. In envied her her outlook. "I just don't worry," she said. "I'm always broke anyways."

Any conversation we could have had was interrupted by several customers. They always came in groups. You would have no one at the checkout lines one minute, then the next, every register would have a line. I thought it might be herd mentality. We were all animals, after all.

This day, our rush of customers probably had to do with the weather. The first snowstorm of the season was predicted. People wanted to get their groceries before the snow hit. They wanted to make sure they had snow brooms for their cars and shovels for their paths. We did sell a few snowblowers for the driveways, but this was mainly plow country. Go outside in the winter and you'd see a good share of pickup trucks with plows attached sitting in the parking lot. My neighbor took pity on me and plowed my parking area for me after most storms, so I wouldn't have to use my snowblower. I only had to shovel my walk and rake the snow off my roof. I was grateful, because I was too exhausted after working at Big Box to want to do any more work than that. But I dreamed of someday having a snowplow and pickup of my own. The storms also brought out the friendliness in our customers. The weather was harsh enough that people knew they needed to help each other.

Kim and I were busy. We typed a code into our registers to signal the managers that we needed help. The trouble was, with the store cutting back hours, this year even as Christmas approached, there was no one to help us. As the lines were beginning to thin, a manager appeared at the register beside us. "Finally," one of the customers muttered. "Now they send somebody," another said. Customers routinely complained about the long lines. The store's answer was to add cashiers and cut back on the hours given the existing cashiers. A good portion of the new cashiers quit in the first week or two, leaving the store less staffed than before the hirings. For a few weeks, the store would bump up the hours it gave the original cashiers, then there would be new hirings and the cycle would start again.

We suspected that the tendency was to give more recent hires most of the hours because they made a slightly lower wage than veteran employees. We also suspected that the store was taking a tax credit for creating jobs. We were skeptical when part of a federal jobs stimulus package was proposed to include incentives for employers to cut hours for existing workers so the employers could hire the unemployed. As we knew all too well, we existing workers could barely make ends meet as it was, say nothing about cutting our hours further. A couple of cashiers tried to send email to the Department of Labor voicing their concerns, but the email bounced back to them. Finally, they typed a letter and mailed it to the department. I was amazed that the cashiers persisted. Surely, our federal government needed to know the pressures faced by the working class. But it took our cashiers more effort to make their opinions known than I imagined it took the moneyed class.

Many of the cashiers didn't own computers because they could not afford the computers. If they did own a laptop, they usually had to go to a public library or a local business that offered free wireless Internet access because they either couldn't afford high speed Internet access at home or the service was not available in their remote, rural location. The situation, of course, was especially challenging for cashiers who had school-aged children. Students had to do much of their work at local libraries and at the school. Around the country, some municipalities were cutting back on libraries' hours of operation to save money. Mercifully, our local communities recognized the necessity of libraries and were maintaining hours. Still, each year there was pressure to cut funding to public libraries. The working poor faced many pressures in many aspects of their lives. I struggled. I watched my coworkers struggle. The gulf between the well-paid and the working poor had grown wide since the 1970s, when my father was a well-paid union autoworker.

I looked at Kim, one register down from me, moving with speed to ring up and bag a customer's purchases, chatting with the customer in her friendly manner. Surely, she deserved better pay than she was getting. Surely, I did. And surely, the companies, which posted billions of dollars in profit annually, could afford to pay all their workers at least a decent, living wage. There were many injustices the poor faced, from substandard schools (the state had evaluated the preparedness of high school graduates for college and found only 22 percent were ready in the school district in which I lived) to a lack of affordable health care, but the most basic seemed to me to be pay. If some of the inequality in wages in this country were reduced, life would become much less hard for many people. It was a social justice issue.

I kept ringing out my customers. In a hurry, I slammed my finger hard against the upright portion of the scanner. We had to be careful. We were moving so fast that we often got bruises. We were constantly breaking our fingernails, even though we kept them trimmed short. We worked in an atmosphere where the air was dry and we were constantly touching items, so our hands dried out and often cracked, giving an entryway for germs. I put lotion on my hands several times a day and applied petroleum jelly at night. I managed to keep my fingers from cracking. But I had quite a few bruises.

Finally, there was a lull. The manager, who had taken about five customers, left. Kim and I had lost count of how many customers we had waited on during the rush. Kim went looking for spray cleaner so we could get the mess off our conveyor belts. Invariably, a jug of milk would have leaked on another jug on the shelf below it, which would mean the leaked-on jug that the customer picked up would have left a ring of milk on the conveyor belt when the customer set down the milk. The raw chicken was worst. The packages almost always leaked. Sometimes, the hamburger and steak packages leaked, too. Whenever we saw chicken juice or beef blood on the conveyor belt, we would try to stop the belt and clean it. But the fast belts often moved along before we could stop them. It was amazing how fast the belts got dirty. We were supposed to have paper towels and cleaner at each register, but we seldom did. We complained often, but the managers rarely responded. On break, I'd sometimes ask Willard for supplies. He'd sneak them to us, in between cleaning the restrooms.

Willard cleaned each of the five restrooms every two hours. He also collected cans and bottles from the machines in the foyer. Our state collected a nickel deposit on soda, beer and water containers. He also swept and mopped the floors. If a customer dropped a glass jar of tomato sauce and it smashed, Willard was usually the one to clean it up, because we cashiers had to keep ringing up the rest of the customer's goods and then run to get a replacement jar of sauce. In the winter, Willard shoveled snow. And of course, he was paid less than we cashiers. He also worried that the store was about to cut his hours. Willard was among the few workers who was scheduled 40 hours each week. Since he and his sisters helped support their parents, he was especially worried.

We were all worried as soon as we started getting snow. The store's roof was flat, even though residential construction was required by state and local laws to have a significant pitch on the roof to accommodate the heavy snow load that our area received. The first winter it was open (the store opened in August, just in time for back-to-school shopping), a steel support beam buckled and workers saw a crack in another beam. The news media reported that the cracked beam was discovered in the morning. But longtime employees said they saw it at 10 p.m. the night before and reported it to the night manager. Employees came to work by 7 a.m. the next day. Customers and employees were evacuated two hours later, 11 hours after the cracked beam was discovered, according to the employees.

The buckled beam was discovered by firefighters shopping in the evening. Employees who were working at the time told me the night manager again ignored the problem. Customers called the police, who contacted the local building inspector and evacuated the building.

Both beams were repaired. The roof continued to pass inspection. Managers daily measured snow on the roof and often had the snow shoveled off by hand. There was never a collapse, although several hard winters had passed.

But the roof continually leaked. Willard got buckets ready to spread around the store when it started raining. About two hours after the rain started, the leaks would start, he knew. Customers often slipped on rain-covered floors. Employees sometimes slipped.

During the winter, all the employees watched the beams for signs of stress and planned their evacuation routes if they saw any trouble. Though we looked out for our customers, we planned to abandon our stations, head to our lockers to get our belongings and flee the building long before an evacuation might be declared. We never felt completely safe in the winter. Despite the roof's problems, the managers had told us employees that the company would not replace the roof. Replacing it would be too expensive. Crews often got on the roof to patch it, but as soon as one leak was fixed, another would spring. Some areas, no matter how often they were patched, continued to leak. I wondered how much the steel had rusted. The heating and cooling equipment was housed just below the roof. Had water leaked around electrical components? How much wear could the steel take and still support the equipment and the roof? By the time I left, the roof had endured nine years of leaking. Store sales were down and some employees wondered privately if the company planned to close the store in a year or two. Since this store had opened, the chain had opened other stores within a 20-mile radius. We wondered how many employees would be transferred and how many would lose their jobs. We wondered a lot. Although we probably had more job security than many during those lean economic times -- our grocery business was pretty good -- we knew we could easily be fired. "No matter how long we've been here and how good our record is, if we do something wrong and they want to get rid of us, they will, just like that," Kim said, snapping her fingers.

It was nearly lunchtime, thank God. My back was killing me. No one had come to relieve me, so I stayed at the register, knowing I'd be saved by the computer's lockout program. When you were 10 minutes late for lunch, the register would flash a message "approaching operator lockout." At 15 minutes late, the message would change to "please sign off." At 20 minutes late, as soon as you finished a transaction, you would be knocked off the system. Longtime cashiers told me they were forever late for lunch before the system was instituted a couple of years before I came to Big Box. The lockout system also served as a great way to clear a line, about as effective as getting a customer who participated in the federal Women, Infants and Children nutrition program. Our state was one of the few that still used paper coupons for WIC. Children up to age 5 and pregnant or nursing women were eligible. They received monthly coupons for free infant formula, legumes, peanut butter, tuna, eggs, cereal, juice and a slew of dairy products, as well as fresh, canned and frozen produce. I suspected the items were chosen by the government not so much for nutrition but to satisfy powerful lobbies, such as the dairy industry. As a vegan, I cringed at the amount of milk and cheese pushed on people who were of low enough income to qualify for the program. The catch on getting the food was that the customer had to get exactly the item specified in exactly the size specified or the store would be denied payment. The store didn't want to lose money, so it made us cashiers be exact. Two of the managers during my tenure had times when they would insist that a low-level manager be called to conduct the WIC transaction because they didn't trust the cashiers, most of whom knew the WIC program better than the managers.

These times were my biggest complaint at Big Box. I had been a copy editor for many years, editing murder stories and stories that were potentially libelous. But I couldn't be trusted to perform a WIC transaction? It was insulting and demeaning to stand with a line of customers and wait for a manager "to do it right." I often reminded the managers of my career as a print journalist, but it was to no avail. I was still treated as though I were illiterate. Fortunately, many customers had complained about the wait, and the manager who was currently overseeing the cashiers was letting us do our own WIC transactions. "We know how to do it better than the managers anyway," Kim commented, reading my mind. She was right. We often had to tactfully correct a manager who was about to let a customer get an improper item. When we did the transactions, it was no problem. But it meant we would sometimes have to leave the register to get the appropriate item. The other customers would wait, or flee to another line. Similarly, when we said the computer was about to lock us out, the customers would head elsewhere. They made me think of Willard's dates, who lost interest in him as soon as they learned he cleaned toilets at Big Box.

Emma arrived just as I got the "please sign off" message. Always conscientious, Emma was apologizing for being late coming back from break, but she had been sent to her break late in the first place. I was famished, but glad to go a little late because it would make the afternoon shorter. I also thought I might be timed to meet WIllard in the lunchroom. Like Kim, his outlook encouraged me.

As we settled into our seats at the plastic lunch table, I looked admiringly at Willard's pasta primavera. "Tell me again why you left cooking for Big Box," I prompted him. "Actually, I left cooking for Fire and Home Insurance Co.," Willard said, taking a bite of broccoli. Turns out Willard had worked five years for the insurance company but had been laid off when the economy took a downturn. "I didn't know that," I said. There were many things none of us knew about each other, or would only find out after years of working together. Willard had lost his middle-class income and his benefits with the job loss. Not wanting to return to the culinary world, where job prospects were slim and hours were long, he opted for cleaning toilets and sweeping floors at Big Box. "At least I have health insurance now," he said. But it had been hard for him to think of himself as a custodian instead of an insurance agent. Like so many people whose professional jobs disappeared during the Great Recession, Willard had largely defined himself by his work. I understood. After I left the newspaper, despite the support of family and friends, for a time I felt worthless. A neighbor had told me how, when the china maker she worked for closed the local factory, sending work that had been performed locally for 150 years overseas, a coworker had been devastated. The china maker was the one that years earlier had refused work to Inga, an immigrant with experience hand-painting top-of-the-line china. The coworker, who through the years had become my neighbor's friend, became depressed. She couldn't find work. She felt that she no longer contributed to society. One day, she killed herself. Coming to Big Box was a courageous move for Willard. I didn't think I knew many professionals who would do it. Then I thought of how many former professionals worked at Big Box. Perhaps that was why I liked these people so much. They were a hardy bunch. They were survivors and, for all their kindnesses and gentleness, they were fighters. They never completely lost hope. They made up the fabric of America.

I wondered if Willard had had such a problem finding a date when he worked at the insurance company. But, as I told him, if a woman didn't want to have dinner with him because he was a janitor at Big Box, she wasn't worth seeing anyway. "It just weeds out the ones who aren't worth your time," I told him. His sisters kept at him to leave Big Box. "But with the economy the way it is, I'm better off staying here," he said. He had a short commute. He was one of the few workers who had regular hours. "And my job at the insurance agency is never going to come back," Willard said.

Lunchtime was almost over. Willard left to call home and check on his parents. Then he would shovel the entrance to the store. It had started snowing. One of our coworkers told us when she came in for work and stopped by the lunchroom to put her lunch in one of the refrigerators. With no windows in the room, our only clue as to what the weather was like came when we could hear the wind shake the roof panels. Fortunately, it wasn't windy, or visibility would have been near zero. The wind and snow often combined to make driving treacherous. I thought about Inga and her eyesight problems, about Maxine and her remaining cataract. Today, we were lucky. I headed back to the register.

I was assigned to a speedy checkout near the door. Madelyn was doing a stint as a greeter. She was wearing a hooded sweatshirt over a sweatshirt over a polo shirt. We weren't allowed to wear hats in the store or she would have had one on, I'm sure. "I wish I'd brought gloves," she said. "I'm glad it isn't windy." When the wind whipped outside, it would come through the double doors every time a customer entered or exited. We cashiers took to wearing vests, so our arms wouldn't be overly burdened by layers. I usually had hot tea for lunch, but not too much, lest I have to use the ladies room when I had a line of customers. I often wondered why the store didn't install a set of interior doors to conserve heat in the winter and cool air in the summer. The store was often hot in the summer and cold in the winter during my first two years working there. Customers' ice cream was practically soup when they checked out in July. The last two years, it was cold all year. We supposed that the cooler temperatures preserved the produce better and made the coolers and freezers more efficient. But in the winter, some of the customers complained it was cold, and they were wearing winter coats. I was glad we didn't have to stock the freezers. Our hands got cold enough ringing up our customers' frozen items.

The store had been advertising that it accepted manufacturers' coupons, so we were getting an onslaught of customers with multiple coupons. Often, the customers hadn't purchased the right item or enough of the items to qualify for the coupons. Usually, the customers were angry when we politely told them of their mistake. Sometimes they argued. Sometimes they demanded to see a manager, as though magically the meaning of the words on the coupon would change when a manager appeared. I came close to telling the customers that I had been a copy editor and perhaps knew better than they did what the words meant. But I doubt it would have mattered. These customers would look at the person behind them in line and shrug, as though saying, "What can I do? This cashier is stupid!" I got several such customers that afternoon. Sometimes I thought the customer was just trying to get away with something. Sometimes I thought the customer really did have a reading comprehension problem. I wondered how much business the store was gaining by attracting more coupon-clipping and coupon-downloading customers. Did the store realize the frustration it was causing the cashiers? Did the store care? Obviously, it did not. Would Dean Bliven have approved?

I was relieved when I saw Emma coming to take my place. "I hope you brought your vest," I said. "I just called Earl on my break and he said there's been accidents nearby. Be careful when you drive home," Emma told me. Emma was sweet; she always worried about me driving home alone. But occasionally I wasn't alone. Tonight I was dropping Kim off at her home in the trailer park.

The next morning dawned bright and beautiful. The snow was white and clean. The sky was a deep, cloudless blue. The air was crisp. The roads were clear, and I enjoyed the drive to Big Box, though I would rather have been skiing or hiking in the December snow. I had an early shift. I was scheduled to relieve Amber for her first break. Amber was waiting to hear from her mother and sister about her other sister, who was expecting a baby any moment. "They left for the hospital this morning," she said. She was eager to get back to the lunchroom so she could check her cellphone for messages. Amber's sister had dismayed their parents by announcing her engagement on a social networking Internet site before she had told her family. The family wasn't fond of the fiance. The couple had married and had an apartment. Thanks to heath care reform, they had medical insurance under her parents' plan. Only Amber, being employed at Big Box, wasn't eligible. At least it meant the new mother and her baby would have good coverage.

Amber was excited about becoming an aunt, but she remained disappointed that she couldn't find a decent job, having gone to college and done everything "right." She listened to politicians talk about the necessity of getting a college degree and heard them cite numbers that showed employment higher for college graduates than for those with only a high school diploma. But those numbers didn't show how many people with college degrees were underemployed -- working in dead-end jobs with little pay. Amber didn't even need a General Equivalency Diploma to work as a cashier. Neither did I. But at least I had spent 21 years working in my field of choice. Aside from volunteering on a local political campaign and running her own current campaign for town council, Amber hadn't had that satisfaction. Neither had many of the other young cashiers at Big Box and elsewhere. I worried about these people. I worried about them personally and about the loss of talent to our society. How could our country compete in the contemporary, global market if so much of its talent was voiceless, trapped at Big Box?

Amber was back from her break. She stopped by my register to let me know that her sister was progressing through labor nicely. She expected to be an aunt by the afternoon. She was excited. So was my customer. She was one of the pleasant customers, who seemed to become fewer all the time. She congratulated Amber and briefly told us about the birth of her son two years before. Emma and Kim overheard and were excited. Amber rushed to her register. She was already late signing onto the computer. Although the manager on duty was understanding, there would be consequences for us all if our computer login times weren't what they were supposed to be. We would be watched every second, sent to complete mindless tasks, perhaps have a note put in our personnel file.

These computer times were apparently so important that the managers often had us fake them. We learned a way to sign on to a register as though we were running. If we pushed a certain series of buttons, we would stay signed on, even past the 15 minutes of inactivity that would normally automatically sign us off and the lunchtime lockout function. In this way, the registers would appear to be well staffed while half the cashiers were off stocking shelves or folding clothes. This trick worked so well that cashiers would even clock out for the day yet remain a phantom at the register. One cashier came in one morning to find herself still signed on from the night before. I wondered if the district managers would catch on to the scheme.

I suppose if you're not allowed to use your creativity at work in regular ways, you'll put it to use somehow, coming up with bizarre ways to pretend cashiers were ringing out customers when they weren't. But we would have to stop our charade soon. It was December, after all, and at least on the weekends, we would be getting holiday shoppers. This season, though, hadn't started out well. Black Friday had been a disappointment. It was rumored that we again wouldn't be getting our quarterly bonuses, which were due that month. We no longer expected the bonuses, but we kept hoping that miraculously we might get another one some quarter.

We all just wished Christmas would be over. We were starting to get the do-gooder shoppers buying clothing for children whose families were of low income. Some of these people were fine and seemed to sincerely want to help people who were less fortunate financially. Others continually questioned us as to whether the parents could exchange the items for other items. I think they were afraid the parents would hock their children's gifts to buy beer and cigarettes. This could happen, but we reminded the customers, who usually proudly announced to us which church they belonged to, that the parent might need to return the item because it might not fit the child, even though it was the child's usual size. We suggested gift receipts. The customers dithered. "I'll give you one anyway, then you can decide whether to include it in the package," I told one customer, who was holding up a long line. I grew to despise do-gooders. If Jesus comes again, I thought, he or she will be a cashier. And he or she will again be crucified beside thieves, after having been falsely accused of stealing a returned piece of merchandise at Big Box. When would this holiday season end?

The trouble was, we knew January would bring high heating bills and fewer hours. The first year I was at Big Box, several of the greeters, who were retired from their regular jobs, took time off to go to the southern states during the winter. I immediately signed up for their shifts. It was boring and cold at the door, and customers were grumpy when, as required, I asked to see their receipts, but it gave me a few more hours of work. I admit, though, that I asked for receipts only often enough to avoid suspicion from the managers. Frankly, unlike the rest of the greeters, I didn't care if the customers walked off with half the store. The last year I worked there, Big Box changed its policy and told the greeters they would have to quit and file to be rehired if they wanted their winters off. Naturally, they would be rehired at a lower pay rate. And January was a slow month, so the store could have spared the greeters for a month or two. Several of the greeters quit.

In February, business started picking up, if only slightly, as some people got money back from the government after filing their income taxes. We would have the last-minute Valentine's Day rush when we would sell hundreds of bouquets of flowers as well as the vases that we hadn't been able to get rid of on clearance sale. One manager came up with the idea of putting flowers in vases and selling them for a higher price than either the flowers or the vase would command alone. It worked. We cleared out of vases and flowers. We cleared out of candy. We sold countless greeting cards. February 15, the store looked like a ghost town. It would be quiet until the Easter season.

The deli got fish for Lent. We sold a lot. We seemed to sell a lot of greasy, fried, fattening food -- chicken and mozzarella sticks. Many of our customers were overweight. We did a big business in the pharmacy. Many of our customers were not in the best of health. Despite the chain pledging to sell healthy, fresh produce at a good price in the interests of its customers' health, most of our produce remained overpriced and of inferior quality.

The exception was greens, which we sold for the best price I could find in our region. I had to give credit where credit was due. I always bought my greens at Big Box.

One of the deli workers warned us to stay away from the rotisserie chicken. Although the cooker had just passed an inspection by the county health department, it smelled bad. The worker suspected a piece of chicken had fallen somewhere inaccessible and rotted. "You don't want to get within three feet of it," she said. The deli workers also advised us which days to order fried foods, since the oil was changed only about once a week. I felt fortunate to be vegan. At least I could count on the greens.

What was out of sight, like the probable rotting piece of chicken, always worried us. We tried to keep our hands clean, but with the volume of traffic we got in the confined space of the store, germs were all around us. The merchandise was constantly dusty, even though we dusted several times a day. Some of the employees who had worked in retail many years said you developed an immunity to most germs, which may have been true. In my first year at Big Box, I got several sinus infections and of course didn't dare try to take time off. I nursed myself with goldenseal, a natural antibiotic. Subsequent years were better. I escaped the flu that sent many employees rushing for the nearest trash can in which to hurl.

SPRING

Spring was coming. We had a rush of flower and candy sales again at Easter. While our Christmas clientele had been grumpy, our Easter customers were decidedly nicer. Did they, too, think Jesus would return as a cashier?

Those of us who didn't have young children switched shifts with the ones who did so they could spend Easter morning with their youngsters. Instead of seeing sunrise with a church congregation, we saw it at Big Box, provided we were lucky enough to be assigned to a register near the plate-glass doors. I suppose we few cashiers that morning made a congregation of our own. Kim and Emma were with their grandchildren. Willard would have liked to have been with his nieces, but he couldn't afford to take time off, even if the managers had approved it. I was stuck at a register in the middle of the bank of checkout lanes every Easter I was at Big Box. But Willard, who managed to be sweeping by the doors each Easter sunrise, told me it was beautiful.

The after-church crowd was pleasant on Easter, unlike most other times of the year. People stopped in to buy dessert and some more flowers. It slowed at dinnertime. Another holiday was behind us. How profitable had it been? Probably not enough to assure a now-rare bonus. We grew to genuinely dislike holidays. Having come from a newspaper, I was used to working holidays, so it wasn't that bad for me. But for some employees, especially those who were retired and hoped to spend their golden years with at least some leisure, it was hard. It was sad that they had to work, that their pensions had vanished or had come up short, that their Social Security checks didn't cover their modest living expenses. Yet some of our customers obviously had generous retirement income, though they sometimes complained that they didn't. These were the ones whose pensions we could look up online at the library, the ones who had been public employees. These people were not harder workers, smarter or more educated than the Big Box workers. They were just more fortunate. I was again annoyed and dismayed by the inequality. It was grating on my nerves. I watched Maxine working, her oxygen tank resting in a shopping cart beside her. I remembered Earl struggling to catch his breath while he bagged for me. These people weren't working because they were bored. They were working because they had to financially. Jesus will come back as a cashier, I thought again.

We opened the garden center. The days were lengthening and the temperature was rising. We did a brisk business in mulch, topsoil, fertilizer, plants, even some lawn mowers. We began to hope that we might again see a bonus in our checks. The town in which I lived was going through a property value reassessment. I owned an older property, which hadn't changed assessed value in many years, and I was afraid my assessment would rise. A larger home value would have been good if I had wanted to sell my home, but I just wanted to be able to afford to live there for the rest of my life. Homeowners in neighboring towns had seen their property taxes double. How could I afford double the property taxes on my Big Box income, which in effect was falling because of the lack of quarterly bonuses? I was worried. I had savings, but I knew those savings would go fast if I had to begin dipping into them. What were my options in a bad economy?

The customers complained that our plants weren't watered.

"It's getting to me," I told Kim one warm spring day. "I keep just wanting to quit." I mentally did the arithmetic. How long could I survive on my savings if I didn't find another job right away? Would a few months off be worth quitting? It would take more than a few days or even a few weeks to recover a sense of rest and well-being after slogging away at Big Box six days a week for four years. What if I had to eventually take a job somewhere at $8 an hour? Could I survive on $8 an hour? Did I want to spend the rest of my life working so hard for so little pay, exhausting myself and wearing out my body, chained to a low-pay, dead-end job in the land of the free? Wasn't our freedom marred by economic inequality?

"I know, I know," Kim comforted me until a customer came to her line. "How do you stand it?" I asked her. "I know, I know, it's the fire," I answered my own question. But didn't a woman who had survived a fatal fire, who had fought to regain use of her hands, who now worried that lasting damage to her lungs was catching up with her, didn't she deserve better? Didn't we all? Why were we becoming a nation of the wealthy few, the evaporating middle class and the growing poor? "How can you stand it," I repeated, rhetorically this time.

Just then, thankfully, a customer came. Maybe that was why the managers kept us busy every second, so that these infrequent lulls wouldn't give us time to think about our lot and start planning a revolt -- or a union organizing drive.

Chapter 6

SUMMER AGAIN

I had good customers that afternoon. It was a miracle. Summer was coming. Summer was somewhat like Christmas in that it brought out the worst in our customers. They were impatient. They complained. They insisted a price rang up too high even when it didn't. They were hot. They were tired. They were condescending and rude. Emma was even having trouble keeping up a smiling facade.

Poor Amber. She had just sent out another round of resumes to no avail. Her social networking sites, geared to professionals, weren't giving her any leads. She was thinking of trying to climb the corporate ladder at Big Box, although she hated retail work. And she wasn't sure whether she could even get a good foothold in management. Though Big Box insisted it didn't discriminate, we couldn't help but notice that most of the promotions went to young white men. Often, the women managers were the ones selecting the men. It seemed to me that I read something about that happening, women promoting the people who had been benefiting for years at the expense of women and minorities. These young men had nothing over Amber. She was smart, talented and a hard worker.

We had thunderstorms. The power went out. We cashed out customers as fast as we could before the registers shut down. Then we had to put away the items that we hadn't been able to ring up in time. The sales floor workers wrapped plastic around the coolers to keep the items cold. We didn't know how long the power would be out. We unloaded a truck. At least the work was something different than usual. The store grew hot.

The power came back on, thankfully, after three hours. We reopened. We took the plastic off the coolers and checked the temperatures. The food was still cold.

State health department rules said we couldn't sell the rotisserie chicken. Someone put the chicken in the lounge for the employees to eat. Remembering the warning from the deli worker a few months before, no one would touch it.

The debit card readers weren't working right. Being on backup power had caused a problem. We didn't know when it would be fixed. We advised the customers to run their cards as credit. Many of them swore at us. It was still hot in the store. Thankfully, we didn't get any food stamp customers, because they had to run their benefit cards as debit.

We sold out of air conditioners and were down to a few fans. It was late July; the dog days were upon us. My feet swelled and ached. My back ached. My wrists ached. My neck ached.

"How do you stand it?" I again asked Kim. She was never hot, it had seemed, these years I had worked at Big Box with her. That day she had worn short sleeves.

I realized that I had never seen her in short sleeves. She shrugged. We got a wave of cranky customers.

I heard the greeter yell. One customer had loaded a large plastic tote with electronic items and run out of the store. The greeter, though she wasn't supposed to chase customers, ran after him. Several managers ran after her. The thief dropped the items on the grassy hill near the store and got away. The items didn't appear to be damaged. That was the most excitement we had had since a customer had seen a mouse on the floor in my line one Christmas season. Then, too, the manager had come running, taking apart two registers before she cornered the mouse and, wearing gloves, took it out to the snow-covered hill.

I didn't know what to do. I had spent nearly four years in a job that would not have been so bad had we employees been given better pay, better benefits and a chance to display some creativity. I felt trapped. At least for a few years, I had been part of the middle class and had some savings. I again wondered if I dared quit. What about Kim, Emma, Maxine, Willard and all the others? Could they afford to quit? How did they keep going? How did they maintain a sense of humor? I had lost mine.

I warned some of the low-level managers that I was reaching the point where I couldn't take it any longer. I think having worked in a profession, with freedom, respect and decent pay, I was spoiled. I couldn't stand Big Box for more than four years. The thought I kept returning to was that I shouldn't have to stand a low-wage, low-benefit job. No one should. Unions had organized when workers had it much worse. We at Big Box benefited from reforms that union workers had fought to get for all employees. Maybe in some fields, unions had become greedy, but they were sorely needed at Big Box and many, many other employers in the United States.

"You need a vacation," Kim told me as the last customer in her line left. "Do you have any time coming?"

"I do have a week," I said. "I'm taking it next month when the weather's better." It was August again. The worst of the heat was over. I had been allowed one week of vacation the previous September; it had been my first vacation in three years. But I had spent it catching up on projects I had been too tired to undertake at home when I was working six days a week. I returned to work a little rested, but not much. This vacation I was hoping to rest for at least a couple of days. But it was hard keeping up responsibilities at home, working so many days and worrying whether I would make enough money to make ends meet. So far, I had avoided visiting a food pantry, though most Big Box workers had to.

It had been a long week. It was Saturday. We had a steady stream of customers. I moved as fast as I could. I got some nasty customers, but most of them were decent. I had lunch with Willard, Kim, Emma and Amber. I had my first break with Maxine; my last with Emma. The state fair was bringing us plenty of customers on their way to and from the festivities. I had an early shift the next morning.

ﺍﻟﻟﻟﻟﺍ **Chapter 7**

THE ENDING

That was the fateful morning when I reached the Big Box saturation point. As soon as I clocked in and came to the front of the store where the registers were, I was sent to join Emma stuffing inserts into the Sunday newspaper. This was the newspaper where I had worked as a reporter, editor and page designer for most of my 21 years in journalism. Being sent to stuff inserts into it was the final slap in the face in a long line of insults. Willard walked in. "How we doin'?" he boomed in his ever cheerful, but slightly sarcastic voice. I liked Willard so much. "Oh Willard," I said. "I can't do this." I was fighting tears. He looked shocked. He sent a low-level manager over to me to see what was wrong; she suggested I take some time in the ladies room to compose myself, then return and start putting away merchandise that customers had discarded around the store. In the ladies room, I did the arithmetic one last time. The low-level manager came in to check on me. "Are you OK?" she asked. "Not really," I replied. I left the ladies room, walked into the store manager's office and resigned. I had never left a job without giving two weeks' notice. I was fortunate. The store manager took one look at my face, asked no questions and filled out my termination paperwork. She listed me as eligible to be rehired. I was leaving for personal reasons. The company would give me a neutral reference if asked by another potential employer.

Again, I was fortunate. Miraculously, I saw an advertisement for an editing job three days after I walked off the job at Big Box. I was hired. I had wanted at least a month to rest, preferably two. I got a month. I felt drained. The work at Big Box had been physically and emotionally exhausting. I woke up one morning a few days after I quit and just laid in bed, lacking the energy to move an inch. I laid there for an hour or so before I felt strong enough to get up. Most people simply didn't realize how exhausting these supposedly low-skill jobs were. I had never felt so drained in my 21 years as a journalist.

During the morning meeting one summer day a month before I left Big Box, the managers were discussing employee safety. If the company could avoid fines, medical bills and other costs associated with accidents, we employees would have a better chance of seeing a quarterly bonus, the manager told us. Apparently, we were seen as more motivated by money -- maybe $130 for the quarter the way bonuses were going those days --- than our own safety. We also had to be careful of customers getting into accidents. Besides not wanting someone to be hurt, the store had to pay medical bills when customers were injured. We were having the meeting in the produce area, a site of many slip-and-fall accidents thanks to dropped grapes on the floor and, although the manager didn't mention it, the leaky cooler where the cut flowers were placed. Although we employees had complained about the cooler several times, nothing had been done to repair or replace it. The manager also neglected to mention the roof, which began leaking, dripping water onto the floor, about two hours after rain started.

The district management team had been visiting the store more often lately than usual. We employees suspected the reason was the increase in accidents. "If you see any district managers walking around, let us know," one of our managers said. Apparently the district managers didn't always check in with the local managers before inspecting the store. "Also, if you see anyone in here taking pictures or taking notes, let us know," the manager said. "No one is supposed to be doing that."

I thought about the mental notes that I took every day. This manager was relatively new and hadn't been around when I was hired. He didn't know what my job before coming to Big Box had been. I smiled.

Kim, Emma and Earl, Willard, Amber, Maxine, Herbert and Cassie, Madelyn and Gary, Inga and all the others were too busy and exhausted to tell the world how hard we worked for so little. I had once made my living telling the stories of people like them -- now my coworkers, my friends. I had become one of them, and I had no intention of keeping quiet.